KT-525-998

Contents

Who was Jackson Pollock?

▲ The Pollock family enjoying watermelons in Phoenix, Arizona, c.1914-15.
From left to right: Roy, Frank, Charles, Jackson, Jay, Sande and Stella.

Jackson Pollock was one of the first art superstars. He was the leading Abstract Expressionist, one of a group of United States-based artists who found success in the late 1940s.

Pollock's method of splattering paint on to canvas earned him the nickname Jack the Dripper. Amazingly, the drip paintings that made his reputation were all created within a few, busy years.

EARLY LIFE

Nothing in Pollock's boyhood hinted at his future. His parents were of Scottish-Irish descent, and struggled to make a living. Pollock was their fifth and last son, and he was born in Cody, Wyoming on 28 January 1912. Pollock often mentioned his birthplace in interviews, although the family left Cody when he was ten months old. The town was named after 'Buffalo Bill' Cody and stood for all that was wild about the Western frontier – lawlessness, freedom and opportunity.

TIMELINE ▶

1912	1916	1920	1922	1928
Pollock is born in Cody, Wyoming.	Pollock loses a fingertip while chopping wood.	Pollock's father moves away.	Charles enrols at the Otis Art Institute, Los Angeles.	Pollock enrols at Manual Arts High School.